PANDIT GANGARAM

D0128852

I'LL DO ANYTHING YOU SAY.
FOR THE NEXT TWO DAYS, WHENEVER ANYONE CALLS YOU PANDIT, SHOUT AND YELL AT HIM ANGRILY.
WHY SHOULD I DO THAT? I LIKE BEING CALLED PANDIT.
DON'T ARGUE. DO AS I SAY.
YES, BIRBAL SAHIB.
WHERE DO YOU LIVE?
BARA CHOWK, SECOND LANE. FOURTH HOUSE.
NEXT DAY BIRBAL WENT TO THAT ADDRESS. HE FOUND SOME SMALL BOYS PLAYING OUTSIDE. HE CALLED ONE ASIDE—
DO YOU KNOW GANGARAM WHO LIVES IN THAT HOUSE?
YES. HE SCOLDED US YESTERDAY BECAUSE WE WERE MAKING A LOT OF NOISE.
I'LL TELL YOU HOW TO GET EVEN. JUST CALL HIM 'PANDITJI'.
SURE ENOUGH, AS SOON AS THE BRAHMIN STEPPED OUT—
PANDITJI

REMEMBERING BIRBAL'S WORDS, GANGARAM POUNCED ON THE BOY.
YOU... HOW DARE YOU CALL ME THAT.
NOW THE OTHER BOYS TOOK UP THE CUE.
PANDITJI!
OHH PANDITJI!
EACH TIME THEY SHOUTED, GANGARAM WOULD CHASE THEM, BRANDISHING HIS STICK.
WAIT TILL I CATCH YOU!
IT BECAME A POPULAR PASTIME IN BARA CHOWK.
YOU WANT TO HAVE SOME FUN? JUST CALL THAT MAN 'PANDITJI'.
SOON, HOWEVER, THEY TIRED OF THE GAME BECAUSE GANGARAM STOPPED ABUSING THEM.
THE GAME STOPPED, BUT THE NAME STUCK.
I HAVE TO GIVE THESE SWEETS TO GANGARAM IN THIS STREET. WHICH IS HIS HOUSE?
DON'T YOU KNOW PANDITJI'S HOUSE? HERE IT IS!

AND CURRY OF COURSE

AKBAR WAS IMMENSELY PLEASED.
WAH! BIRBAL. YOU ARE INDEED GREAT. HERE! TAKE THIS PEARL NECKLACE.
THE COURTIERS PRESENT WERE PERPLEXED.
WHY, THE KING MUST REALLY BE FOND OF CURRY. HE GAVE BIRBAL A PRESENT JUST FOR MENTIONING THE WORD CURRY.
AFTER THE COURT HAD DISPERSED, THEY GOT TOGETHER FOR DISCUSSIONS.
WE MUST BRING THE BEST CURRY FOR THE EMPEROR TOMORROW.
YES, LOTS OF IT.
SURELY HE WILL REWARD US TOO.
THE NEXT DAY THEY ARRIVED IN THE DURBAR WITH THEIR SERVANTS CARRYING HUGE URNS OF CURRY ON THEIR HEADS.
WHAT'S ALL THIS? WHAT ARE THESE MEN CARRYING TO THE COURT?
WE HAVE BROUGHT CURRY FOR YOU, JAHANPANAH. WE KNOW NOW HOW MUCH YOU LIKE IT.
AKBAR UNDERSTOOD AT ONCE—
YOU FOOLS! WHAT BIRBAL SAID YESTERDAY WAS IN ANOTHER CONTEXT. AS A PUNISHMENT FOR YOUR STUPIDITY I WILL MAKE YOU EAT ALL THIS CURRY JUST NOW.
FORGIVE US! WE WILL NOT ACT IN HASTE NEXT TIME.
BIRBAL HAD A GOOD LAUGH.

THE ONLY ROOSTER

AKBAR LOVED TO PLAY HARMLESS TRICKS ON BIRBAL—
SO MANY TIMES HAVE I TRIED TO TRAP HIM, BUT HE ALWAYS GETS THE BETTER OF ME.
THIS TIME I WILL GET EVEN WITH HIM.
THE NEXT DAY AT THE COURT, HE SENT BIRBAL ON AN ERRAND. ADDRESSING THE REST OF THE COURTIERS, AKBAR SAID—
HERE IS A BASKET OF EGGS. I WANT EACH ONE OF YOU TO TAKE AN EGG AND KEEP IT HIDDEN.
LATER, WHEN I ASK YOU TO DIVE INTO THE POOL, YOU MUST PRETEND YOU FOUND IT THERE. UNDERSTOOD?
YES, JAHANPANAH
QUEER IDEAS HIS MAJESTY HAS.
BETTER HUMOUR HIM AND DO AS HE SAYS.
MUST BE A NEW GAME HE HAS THOUGHT OF.
BUT WHEN BIRBAL RETURNED TO THE COURT, THEY UNDERSTOOD.
BIRBAL, YESTERDAY I HAD A STRANGE DREAM. FROM IT I GOT AN EXCELLENT IDEA FOR TESTING THE ABILITIES OF THE MEN OF MY COURT.

ALL OF YOU MUST DIVE INTO THE POND IN THE GARDEN.
THE GENUINE MEN WILL FIND AN EGG IN IT. IF YOU COME OUT WITHOUT AN EGG, IT WOULD MEAN YOU ARE NOT RELIABLE.
AHA! THE EMPEROR WANTS TO PUT BIRBAL IN HIS PLACE.
WHAT FUN! EVERY TIME BIRBAL MAKES US LOOK SILLY. TODAY IT IS HIS TURN.
BIRBAL SAW THEM WHISPERING.
SOMETHING IS UP! I AM SURE THE EMPEROR IS UP TO ONE OF HIS TRICKS.
ONE BY ONE, THE COURTIERS DIVED INTO THE POOL.
HERE, JAHANPANAH, I HAVE THE EGG.

ME TOO!
NOW IT'S YOUR TURN, BIRBAL.
I SUPPOSE THERE MUST BE A BASKET OF EGGS AT THE BOTTOM.
WHAT WILL BIRBAL DO? HE HAS NO EGG.
HE'LL BE THE ODD MAN OUT.
SERVES HIM RIGHT. THE POMPOUS FELLOW!
COME ON, BIRBAL!
LET'S SEE YOU AND YOUR EGG.
HURRY UP, BIRBAL.
WHEN HE DIVED IN—
THERE'S NOTHING HERE! HE MUST BE TRYING TO TRICK ME.
BIRBAL CAME OUT EMPTY-HANDED FROM THE POOL.

AFTER SHAKING THE WATER OFF HIS BODY, HE STOOD UP.
COCK-A-DOODLE DOO! COCK-A-DOODLE DOO!
WHERE'S YOUR EGG, BIRBAL? WHAT ON EARTH ARE YOU CROWING FOR?
BIRBAL REPLIED—
SURELY YOU KNOW THAT ONLY HENS LAY EGGS, NOT COCKS.
YOU HAVE A LARGE BROOD OF HENS, HUZOOR.
BUT I AM THE ONLY ROOSTER!
THE COURTIERS FELT VERY EMBARRASSED.
HA HA! TRULY BIRBAL, YOU ARE REALLY ONE OF A KIND!

PARTING OF FRIENDS
ONE DAY, WHILE BIRBAL WAS AWAY ON A MISSION, EMPEROR AKBAR CALLED HIS COURTIERS TOGETHER.
I AM A LITTLE WORRIED ABOUT PRINCE SALIM.
WHY HUZOOR?
HE'S A FINE BOY.
AND SO HANDSOME TOO.
AKBAR INTERRUPTED —
YES, I KNOW HE IS A GOOD BOY, BUT OF LATE, HE HAS FALLEN INTO BAD COMPANY.
OH, YOU MEAN THAT BOY, YASIN?
YES, THAT FELLOW IS NO GOOD.
SALIM HAD LEARNT THE ROYAL DUTIES SO WELL.
I WAS REALLY PROUD OF HIM. BUT NOW ALL HE DOES IS LAZE ABOUT ALL DAY, PLAY CARDS, AND GO FOR SHIKAR.
YES, THAT'S TRUE. BUT HUZOOR, IT IS DIFFICULT TO SEPARATE A 16-YEAR-OLD FROM HIS FRIEND.

THAT IS WHY I AM CONSULTING YOU. AFTER ALL, AS THE PRINCE, HIS FUTURE IS YOUR CONCERN TOO.
WE WILL TRY TO FIND A WAY.
BUT A WHOLE MONTH PASSED. NO ONE COULD THINK OF A PLAN TO CORRECT THE PRINCE.
HUZOOR, SEND YASIN AWAY TO ANOTHER PLACE.
NO, THAT WILL ONLY TURN SALIM AGAINST ME.
WHY NOT TELL SALIM WHAT YOU THINK OF YASIN?
NO, MIRZA, THAT MIGHT MAKE SALIM MORE FOND OF HIM.
WHEN BIRBAL RETURNED FROM HIS TRAVELS, AKBAR TURNED TO HIM FOR HELP.
YOU WANT TO SEPARATE THE TWO YOUNG MEN. WHY, GIVE ME JUST TWO DAYS.
NEXT DAY, AT COURT, BIRBAL CALLED YASIN —
BZZZZ!
ALOUD HE SAID —
NOW, DON'T BREATHE A WORD OF THIS TO ANYONE.
BIRBAL MUST BE GOING CRAZY. HE JUST SAID, "JUST ONE SEED IN EVERY MANGO".

AS SOON AS THE COURT DISPERSED, SALIM RUSHED TO MEET YASIN.
WHAT WAS IT? WHAT SECRET DID BIRBAL TELL YOU?
NOTHING. HE JUST WHISPERED SOME NON-SENSE.
SALIM WAS NOT CONVINCED.
HE COULDN'T HAVE CALLED YOU IN THE DURBAR JUST TO WHISPER NONSENSE.
IT'S TRUE. EVEN I CANNOT UNDERSTAND IT.
BUT SURELY HE MUST HAVE SAID SOME-THING.
ALL RIGHT. IF YOU INSIST. ALL HE SAID WAS "JUST ONE SEED IN EVERY MANGO."
YOU ARE HIDING SOME-THING FROM ME, YASIN. I THOUGHT YOU WERE MY FRIEND.
OF COURSE I AM. I AM TELLING YOU THE TRUTH.
I DON'T BELIEVE YOU, YASIN.
BUT IT IS TRUE. HE SAID JUST THAT. MAYBE HE'S GOING CRAZY.
BUT BIRBAL, WHO WAS SECRETLY OVERHEARING THE CONVERSATION, WAS FAR FROM CRAZY.
YASIN, I DON'T WANT TO TALK TO YOU EVER AGAIN IN MY LIFE.
IF YOU DON'T TRUST ME, I TOO DON'T WANT YOU AS A FRIEND.
AND SOON, SALIM WENT BACK TO HIS ROYAL DUTIES.

THE PHASES OF THE MOON
ONCE AKBAR SENT BIRBAL TO KABUL ON A SECRET ROYAL MISSION.
BIRBAL TRIED TO MINGLE WITH THE LOCAL CROWD, BUT—
I SUSPECT THAT MAN! HE DOESN'T LOOK LIKE AN ORDINARY PERSON.
YES, THOUGH HE POSES TO BE ONE OF US, HE IS OBVIOUSLY AN OUTSIDER.
WHY, HE MUST BE A SPY.
LET'S REPORT HIM TO OUR KING.
THE KING ORDERED THE SUSPECTED SPY TO BE BROUGHT BEFORE HIM.
TELL ME TRULY. WHO ARE YOU? WHY ARE YOU HERE?
I AM JUST A TRAVELLER.
I HAVE TRAVELLED THROUGH MANY KINGDOMS AND ARRIVED HERE.
IS THAT SO?
WELL, SINCE YOU HAVE TRAVELLED SO MUCH AND SEEN SO MUCH OF THE WORLD, TELL ME, WHAT DO YOU THINK OF MY RULE?

BIRBAL PAUSED TO THINK —
YOU ARE LIKE THE FULL MOON. NO PHASE OF THE MOON CAN COMPARE WITH IT FOR GLORY.
THE KING LOOKED PLEASED. AS AN AFTERTHOUGHT, HE ADDED —
AND WHAT OF YOUR OWN KING? WHAT DO YOU THINK OF HIM?
OH HIM! HE IS LIKE THE CRESCENT MOON —THIN AND WEAK.
I AM VERY PLEASED WITH YOU. HERE TAKE THIS BAG OF COINS AS A GIFT.
THANK YOU, SIRE. YOU ARE INDEED KIND.
BIRBAL RETURNED TO DELHI. BUT NEWS OF HIS TRIP HAD REACHED THERE. AT DIWAN-I-KHAS—
TELL ME, HUSSAIN KHAN. WHAT SECRET OF BIRBAL DO YOU POSSESS?
OH, JAHANPANAH! YOU KNOW HE HAD GONE TO KABUL LAST MONTH.
YES, YES, I HAD SENT HIM THERE. SO WHAT?
BUT DO YOU KNOW WHAT HE SAID TO THE KING THERE?
WHAT?

HE PRETENDS TO BE YOUR LOYAL AIDE. BUT WHEN HE WENT TO KABUL HE DECLARED IN THE COURT THERE THAT THE KING OF KABUL WAS LIKE A FULL MOON, WHILE YOU WERE JUST A CRESCENT MOON.
IS THAT SO? I WILL ASK HIM TOMORROW IN THE COURT.
SURE ENOUGH, NEXT DAY—
BIRBAL, I HAVE A SERIOUS CHARGE AGAINST YOU.
ME, JAHANPANAH? WHAT HAVE I DONE?
I HAVE COME TO KNOW THAT IN THE COURT OF KABUL, JUST TO FLATTER THE KING THERE, YOU MADE DEMEANING REMARKS ABOUT ME.
THAT'S NOT TRUE!
TELL ME ON OATH, DID YOU NOT COMPARE ME TO A CRESCENT MOON, AND THE KING OF KABUL TO A FULL MOON?
THAT I DID, SIRE.
HOW DARE YOU, BIRBAL! YOU ARE SUPPOSED TO BE MY MOST LOYAL AIDE.
I DID MAKE THAT COMPARISON, SIRE. BUT DON'T YOU REALISE THAT THE FULL MOON IS DESTINED TO DECREASE IN GLORY AND SIZE?
IT IS THE CRESCENT MOON THAT IS FULL OF PROMISE FOR THE FUTURE. IT WILL GROW IN GLORY DAY BY DAY. DON'T THE MUSLIMS AND HINDUS VENERATE THE MOON OF THE SECOND LUNAR DAY?
I SHOULD HAVE KNOWN BETTER THAN TO SUSPECT YOU, AS USUAL, BIRBAL, YOU WIN.

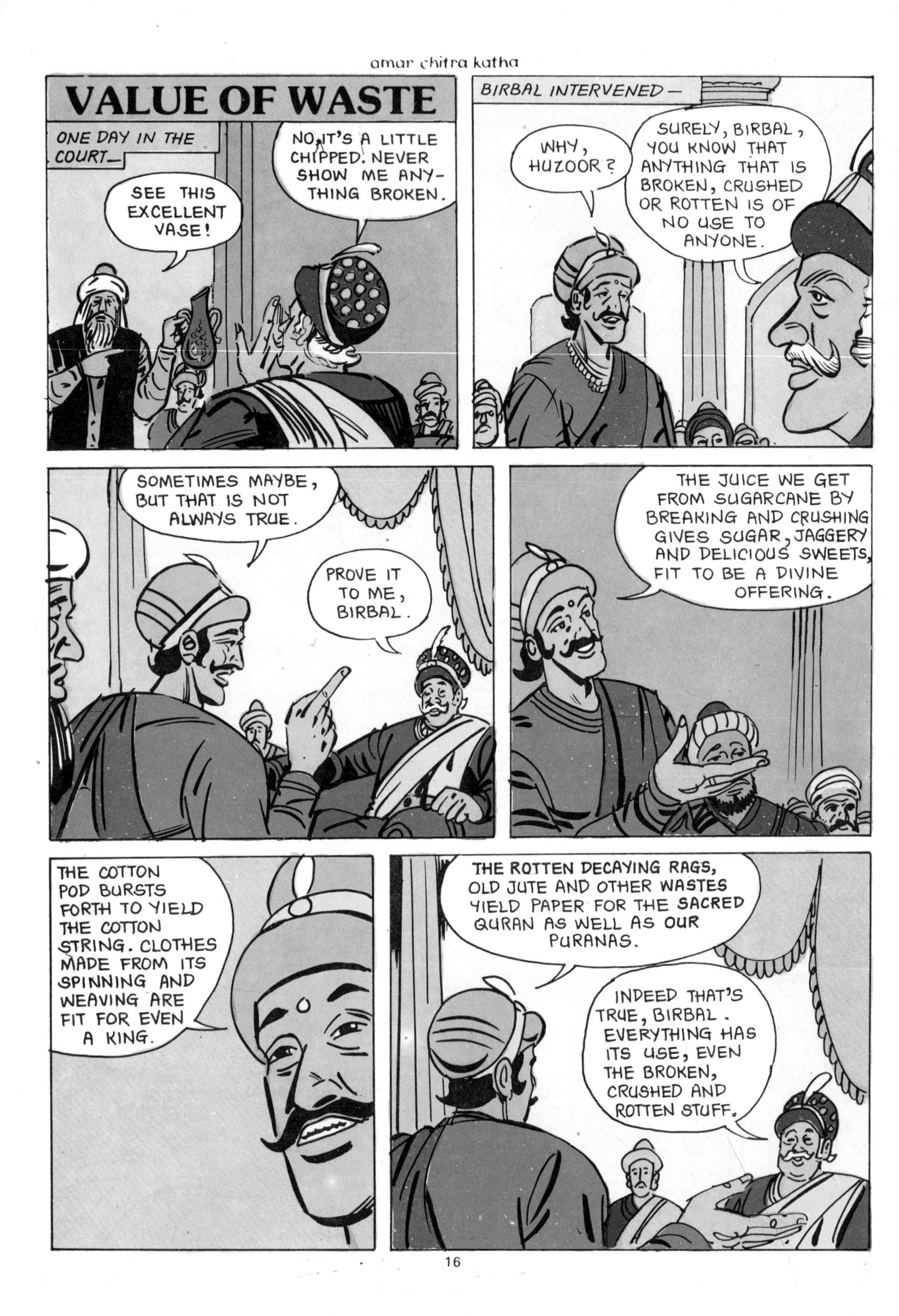
VALUE OF WASTE
ONE DAY IN THE COURT—
SEE THIS EXCELLENT VASE!
NO, IT'S A LITTLE CHIPPED. NEVER SHOW ME ANYTHING BROKEN.
BIRBAL INTERVENED—
WHY, HUZOOR?
SURELY, BIRBAL, YOU KNOW THAT ANYTHING THAT IS BROKEN, CRUSHED OR ROTTEN IS OF NO USE TO ANYONE.
SOMETIMES MAYBE, BUT THAT IS NOT ALWAYS TRUE.
PROVE IT TO ME, BIRBAL.
THE JUICE WE GET FROM SUGARCANE BY BREAKING AND CRUSHING GIVES SUGAR, JAGGERY AND DELICIOUS SWEETS, FIT TO BE A DIVINE OFFERING.
THE COTTON POD BURSTS FORTH TO YIELD THE COTTON STRING. CLOTHES MADE FROM ITS SPINNING AND WEAVING ARE FIT FOR EVEN A KING.
THE ROTTEN DECAYING RAGS, OLD JUTE AND OTHER WASTES YIELD PAPER FOR THE SACRED QURAN AS WELL AS OUR PURANAS.
INDEED THAT'S TRUE, BIRBAL. EVERYTHING HAS ITS USE, EVEN THE BROKEN, CRUSHED AND ROTTEN STUFF.

THE TRUE OWNER

ONE DAY AKBAR, BIRBAL AND THE OTHER COURTIERS WERE IN THE DIWAN-I-AM. SUDDENLY —
HELP ME, HUZOOR.
CALM DOWN! WHAT DO YOU WANT US TO DO?
HUZOOR, I AM A TRADER FROM AFGHANISTAN. I HIRED A BOAT TO BRING MY GOODS HERE. NOW THE BOATMAN CLAIMS THAT HE IS THE OWNER OF MY THINGS.
THOUGH I AM A STRANGER IN THESE PARTS, I KNOW YOUR FAME AS A JUST KING. HELP ME, I BESEECH YOU, I'LL BE A RUINED MAN UNLESS I GET JUSTICE.
BIRBAL, FIND OUT THE FACTS.
AFTER BIRBAL HEARD HIS STORY HE SENT FOR THE BOATMAN AND HIS CREW.
WHY ARE YOU HARASSING THIS TRADER? GIVE HIM BACK HIS GOODS.
HUZOOR, THEY ARE MINE. HE JUST TOOK A RIDE ON MY BOAT. ASK ALL MY OARSMEN.
THE OARSMEN ANSWERED READILY.
YES, THE GOODS BELONG TO OUR SAHIB.

BIRBAL PAUSED FOR A WHILE.
WE'LL SETTLE THE MATTER HERE IN THE COURT TOMORROW.
AFTER THE COURT ADJOURNED, BIRBAL CHANGED HIS COURTIER'S CLOTHES TO THAT OF A MUNIM* AND WENT TO THE RIVERBANK WITH A FRIEND.
THERE, THE SECOND BOAT. HE IS THE MAN. LET'S GO.
AS PLANNED EARLIER, HIS FRIEND BEGAN TO NEGOTIATE.
WHAT GOODS HAVE YOU TO SELL?
OH! THE FINEST PERSIAN CARPETS.
ARE YOU PLANNING TO SELL YOUR THINGS HERE?
YES, IF POSSIBLE. I HAVE GOODS WORTH TEN THOUSAND RUPEES.
WELL, THE MARKET FOR CARPETS IS RATHER LOW IN DELHI THESE DAYS. SO, IF YOU WANT TO SELL YOUR STUFF, I'LL TAKE IT FOR FIVE THOUSAND.
FOR HALF THE PRICE?
THINK ABOUT IT AND LET ME KNOW.
WAIT! WAIT! I'LL SELL IT FOR FIVE THOUSAND.

* A CLERK

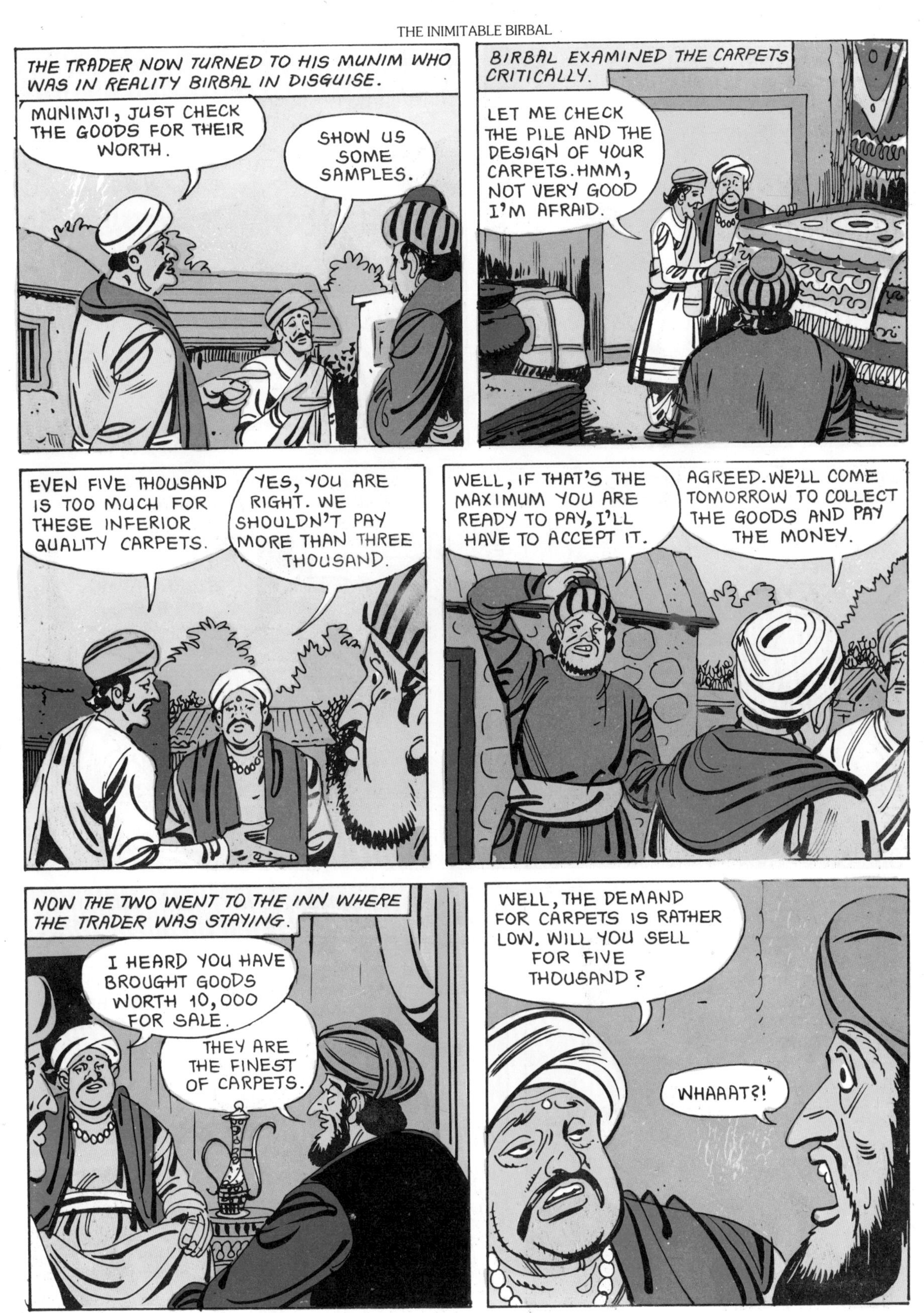
THE TRADER NOW TURNED TO HIS MUNIM WHO WAS IN REALITY BIRBAL IN DISGUISE.
MUNIMJI, JUST CHECK THE GOODS FOR THEIR WORTH.
SHOW US SOME SAMPLES.
BIRBAL EXAMINED THE CARPETS CRITICALLY.
LET ME CHECK THE PILE AND THE DESIGN OF YOUR CARPETS. HMM, NOT VERY GOOD I'M AFRAID.
EVEN FIVE THOUSAND IS TOO MUCH FOR THESE INFERIOR QUALITY CARPETS.
YES, YOU ARE RIGHT. WE SHOULDN'T PAY MORE THAN THREE THOUSAND.
WELL, IF THAT'S THE MAXIMUM YOU ARE READY TO PAY, I'LL HAVE TO ACCEPT IT.
AGREED. WE'LL COME TOMORROW TO COLLECT THE GOODS AND PAY THE MONEY.
NOW THE TWO WENT TO THE INN WHERE THE TRADER WAS STAYING.
I HEARD YOU HAVE BROUGHT GOODS WORTH 10,000 FOR SALE.
THEY ARE THE FINEST OF CARPETS.
WELL, THE DEMAND FOR CARPETS IS RATHER LOW. WILL YOU SELL FOR FIVE THOUSAND?
WHAAAT?!

WELL, SAY SEVEN THOUSAND! COME, IT'S A GOOD PRICE.
NO, NEVER.
NO ONE HERE WILL GIVE YOU MORE THAN THAT. THINK AGAIN.
NEVER MIND. I HAVE BOUGHT THE GOODS FOR TEN THOUSAND. I WILL SELL THEM ONLY AT A PROFIT, NOT OTHERWISE.
NEXT DAY, AT THE APPOINTED HOUR, THE BOATMAN AND THE TRADER CAME TO THE COURT.
SO, WHO IS THE OWNER OF THESE CARPETS?
I, SIR.
NO, THEY ARE MINE.
BIRBAL WAS ALMOST CERTAIN WHO WAS THE TRUE OWNER OF THE GOODS. HE SUMMONED THE OARSMEN TO THE COURT AND CALLED THEM ASIDE.
I KNOW YOUR SECRET. ADMIT, OR ELSE...
AS HE HAD EXPECTED, THE SCARED OARSMEN BLURTED OUT THE TRUTH.
YES SIR, THE GOODS BELONG TO THE TRADER. OUR MASTER GAVE US 25 RUPEES EACH TO SAY THEY WERE HIS. SPARE US!
NOW THAT HIS CRIME WAS OUT, THE BOATMAN QUICKLY CONFESSED—
YES, THAT IS TRUE. I WAS TEMPTED BY THE CHANCE TO MAKE QUICK MONEY.
SINCE IT'S YOUR FIRST OFFENCE. I'LL LET YOU OFF LIGHTLY. YOU MUST RETURN THE GOODS TO THE OWNER AND ALSO PAY HIM RS. 500. TO THE STATE YOU MUST PAY RS. 500 AS FINE.

LIMITS OF LOYALTY
THERE WAS NOTHING AKBAR LOVED MORE THAN CHALLENGING BIRBAL. ONE DAY IN THE COURT —
BIRBAL, I WANT YOU TO FIND THE MOST LOYAL AND THE MOST UNGRATEFUL CREATURE ON EARTH.
YES, HUZOOR.
DON'T JUST SAY YES. YOU MUST PRESENT THEM IN THE DURBAR TOMORROW, OR ELSE...
AS YOU PLEASE.
BIRBAL AGREED TO DO AS ASKED. BUT ON GOING HOME, HIS DAUGHTER SAID —
FATHER, YOU SEEM TO BE WORRIED. YOU'VE BEEN STARING AT THE CEILING FOR THE LAST HALF HOUR.
YES, I AM A LITTLE DISTURBED.
IS IT A PROBLEM POSED BY THE EMPEROR?
YES, HE WANTS ME TO BRING HIM THE MOST LOYAL AND THE MOST UNGRATEFUL CREATURE BY TOMORROW MORNING.

HOW CAN I LOCATE THEM SO FAST?
DON'T WORRY, FATHER. SLEEP PEACEFULLY. I'LL GIVE YOU BOTH THESE IN THE MORNING.
BIRBAL HAD TRUST IN THE MATURE INTELLIGENCE OF HIS DAUGHTER, AND SLEPT SOUNDLY.
NEXT MORNING—
GET READY FOR COURT, FATHER.
BUT THOSE TWO...
ALL YOU HAVE TO DO IS TAKE WITH YOU, YOUR SON-IN-LAW AND OUR DOG, MOTI.
YES. OF COURSE. WHY DIDN'T I THINK OF IT EARLIER?
BIRBAL ARRIVED IN THE DURBAR WITH HIS SON-IN-LAW AND HIS PET DOG.
WHAT IS THIS, BIRBAL? WHY HAVE YOU BROUGHT YOUR DOG? DON'T YOU HAVE ANY RESPECT FOR THE DURBAR?

ON YOUR INSTRUCTIONS, HUZOOR.
MINE?
YES, YOU HAD ASKED ME TO BRING YOU THE MOST LOYAL CREATURE.
SO YOU BROUGHT A DOG?
YES, IF YOU GIVE A STRAY DOG EVEN A MORSEL OF FOOD, HE WILL BE EVER SO GRATEFUL.
HE WILL PROBABLY FOLLOW YOU EVERYWHERE LIKE A SHADOW.
HMM. PERHAPS YOU ARE RIGHT BUT THE OTHER ONE...?
YOU MEAN THE UNGRATEFUL WRETCH. HERE HE IS.
BUT THAT IS YOUR SON-IN-LAW.
YES, HE REPRESENTS ALL SONS-IN-LAW. NO MATTER HOW MUCH YOU GIVE THEM, THEY ARE NEVER SATISFIED.
THAT'S TRUE, BIRBAL.

BUT WE MUST THEN REWARD THE DOG AND PUNISH THE SON-IN-LAW.
LET THE DOG BE FED SUMPTUOUSLY. AS FOR THE SON-IN-LAW, LET HIM BE HANGED.
BUT... BUT... HUZOOR.
NO BUTS, BIRBAL, I BELIEVE IN JUSTICE.
BUT HE IS ONLY A SPECIMEN, ONLY A REPRESENTATIVE OF ALL SONS-IN-LAW.
SO?
IF YOU DECIDE TO AWARD A PUNISHMENT, ALL OF THEM MUST BE HANGED.
WHAT DO YOU MEAN?
I MEAN, YOU WILL HAVE TO HANG ALL SONS-IN-LAW...
...INCLUDING ME AND YOUR ROYAL HIGHNESS. EVERYONE OF US IS SOMEBODY'S SON-IN-LAW.
IN THAT CASE, LET HIM GO!

AND OFF IT FLEW

AKBAR WAS FOND OF STORIES. HE COULD NOT SLEEP UNLESS HE LISTENED TO A NEW TALE EVERY NIGHT.
ONE BY ONE, HIS COURTIERS WOULD BE SUMMONED.
HURRY UP, ASIM. TODAY IT IS YOUR TURN TO TELL A STORY.
AH YES! AND THE KING DOESN'T WANT TO HEAR THE GOOD OLD STORIES. WE MUST TELL NEW TALES TO HIS MAJESTY.
ONE EVENING, IT WAS BIRBAL'S TURN. BIRBAL WOULD SPIN A LONG YARN. EACH TIME HE PAUSED FOR BREATH —
AND THEN?
ALL HE HAS TO SAY IS 'AND THEN?' IT'S MY POOR JAW THAT GETS WEARY TALKING.
I MUST CURE HIM OF THIS HABIT OF HIS. HOW CAN WE FIND END-LESS NEW STORIES EVERY DAY?
BIRBAL WAITED PATIENTLY TILL HIS TURN CAME AGAIN.
COME BIRBAL, I AM FEELING RESTLESS. TELL ME A REALLY LONG STORY TONIGHT.
BIRBAL SETTLED DOWN COMFORTABLY AND BEGAN.
ONE DAY, A RICH FARMER ORDERED A GRANARY TO BE MADE.

HE WANTED THE GRANARY TO BE ABSOLUTELY AIRTIGHT, WITHOUT ANY WINDOW OR VENTILATION.
HMMM.
WHEN THE WHEAT CROP WAS HARVESTED, IT WAS STORED IN THE NEW GRANARY. BUT THERE WAS ONE LITTLE PROBLEM.
WHAT?
HIGH UP ON ONE OF THE WALLS OF THE GRANARY, A SMALL OPENING REMAINED. ONE DAY, A SPARROW CAME, TOOK SOME GRAIN AND FLEW OFF.
THEN?
THEN ANOTHER SPARROW CAME, FILLED HER BEAK WITH GRAIN, AND OFF IT FLEW.
THEN WHAT HAPPENED?
ONE MORE SPARROW MANAGED TO GET IN AND OFF IT FLEW WITH TWO GRAINS OF WHEAT.
BUT WHAT HAPPENED NEXT?
BIRBAL DESCRIBED HOW FIFTY BIRDS HAD GOT INTO THE GRANARY AND FLOWN OFF.
OH COME ON! ENOUGH OF THE SPARROWS PICKING GRAIN!
BUT, JAHANPANAH, THOUSANDS OF BIRDS CAME TO THAT GRANARY. I HAVE MENTIONED ONLY A FEW. ONLY WHEN THE GRANARY IS EMPTY WILL THE STORY MOVE ON.
WHY IT MIGHT TAKE MONTHS OR EVEN YEARS TO COMPLETE THE STORY.
FORGET IT! I DON'T WANT TO HEAR ANY STORIES.

A SHARED DREAM

OH, HOW STRANGE, JAHANPANAH! HOW VERY ODD.
ISN'T IT?
NO. I MEAN I TOO HAD EXACTLY THE SAME DREAM.
REALLY?
YES, BUT I THINK YOU AWOKE BEFORE THE DREAM WAS OVER.
WHY, BIRBAL?
BECAUSE, IN MY DREAM WITH GREAT EFFORT YOU GOT OUT OF THE HONEY PIT.
I TOO MANAGED TO CLAMBER OUT OF THE GUTTER.
AND, THEN, JAHANPANAH! WE BOTH BEGAN TO LICK ONE ANOTHER CLEAN.
OH! OH!

BIRBAL TURNS DETECTIVE

KALU THE ROYAL GARDENER WAS AN ABLE BUT STINGY MAN.
YOU LOOK AFTER THE ORCHARDS SO WELL, KALU.
BUT WHY DO YOU LOOK SO DOWN AND OUT?
OH! I SAVE ALL MY MONEY.
I'M COLLECTING THE MONEY FOR MY OLD AGE.
BUT WHERE DO YOU KEEP IT?
IT'S A SECRET!
ONE DAY KALU CAME IN TEARS TO BIRBAL.
OH, I'M RUINED!
WHAT HAPPENED, KALU?
SOMEONE HAS STOLEN MY LIFE'S SAVINGS!
WHAT?
I HAD STRUGGLED AND SAVED ABOUT A THOUSAND GOLD MOHURS! NOW THEY ARE GONE!
BUT WHERE HAD YOU KEPT THEM?

UNDER A PEAR TREE IN THE ROYAL ORCHARD.
WHY ON EARTH?
WHAT COULD BE SAFER THAN THE ROYAL GARDEN. BESIDES, I SPEND MOST OF MY WAKING HOURS THERE.
DID ANYONE ELSE KNOW ABOUT IT?
NO, NOT A SOUL.
BESIDES I USED TO CHECK IT REGULARLY. I SAW IT JUST TWO DAYS AGO.
BIRBAL PAUSED FOR A MOMENT. THEN—
GIVE ME SOME TIME. I'LL FIND THE THIEF.
WHY SHOULD ANYONE DIG UNDER THAT TREE UNLESS HE KNOWS ABOUT THE TREASURE?
AT LAST—
AH, YES!

BIRBAL CALLED FOR THE LEADING HAKIMS AND VAIDS*
DO YOU USE ANY PART OF THE PEAR TREE TO PREPARE YOUR MEDICINES?
NO!
THE FRUIT IS GOOD FOR HEALTH. BUT WE DON'T USE THE LEAVES OR FLOWERS.
JUST THEN AN OLD AND EXPERIENCED VAID INTERVENED.
YOUR MAJESTY, THERE IS INDEED AN IMPORTANT APPLICATION.
WHY, JUST THE OTHER DAY I CURED A PATIENT OF JAUNDICE IN A CRITICAL STATE USING AN EXTRACT OF THE PEAR ROOTS.
WHO WAS THAT PATIENT?
SETH HAZARIMAL.
BIRBAL SENT FOR SETH HAZARIMAL.
IS IT TRUE THAT VAIDJI TREATED YOU WITH AN EXTRACT OF THE PEAR TREE.
INDEED IT IS. IT SAVED MY LIFE.
WHO FETCHED THE PEAR ROOTS FOR YOU?
MY SERVANT!

* A DOCTOR PRACTISING AYURVEDIC SYSTEM OF MEDICINE.

CALL HIM!
AS YOU WISH.
YOU DUG THE ROOTS OF THE ROYAL PEAR TREE!
YES, HUZOOR.
DIDN'T YOU TAKE THE THOUSAND MOHURS KEPT THERE? FETCH THEM AT ONCE.
I I...
IF YOU CONFESS YOUR CRIME, YOU'LL BE FORGIVEN OR ELSE...
I'LL BRING THE MONEY AT ONCE.
HERE, YOUR EXCELLENCY!
YOU ARE FREE TO GO.
TAKE THESE FIVE MOHURS FOR CONFESSING YOUR CRIME.
BIRBAL TURNED TO KALU—
HERE'S YOUR TREASURE. YOU FORFEITED THE FIVE MOHURS BECAUSE OF YOUR CARELESSNESS.
THANK YOU.
IN FUTURE DON'T DO SILLY THINGS LIKE HIDING YOUR WEALTH IN THE GARDEN.